Getting Physical

The Science of Sports

Deborah A. Parks

SCHOLASTIC INC.

New York   Toronto   London   Auckland   Sydney
Mexico City   New Delhi   Hong Kong   Buenos Aires

Cover Photo
© Jean-Loup Gautreau/Getty Images

Developed by ONO Books in cooperation with Scholastic Inc.

ISBN 0-439-59811-7

5 6 7 8 9 10   23   12 11 10 09 08

Contents

Welcome to This Book 4

1 **Football: Forces to Reckon With** 6

2 **Basketball: A Better Dribble** 11

3 **Baseball: Watching for a Good Pitch** 16

    Athletes' Feet 21

4 **Tennis: What a Racket** 22

5 **Swimming: No Resistance** 27

6 **Marathon Running: Going the Distance** 32

    Fight or Flight? 37

7 **Climbing: Reaching New Heights** 38

    Feeling the Pressure 43

8 **Skateboarding: Going Airborne** 44

9 **Speed Skating: Getting an Edge** 49

Glossary 54

Index 56

Welcome to This Book

Do you want to run faster? Do you want to hit harder? Do you want to reach new heights? You can if you know a little science.

Don't laugh. Some of the top pros in every sport understand the science behind what they do. They know how to make a tackle without breaking their bones. They know what kind of fuel their body needs to run a marathon race. They know how to use their weight to catch big air on a skateboard.

Science can help you get game, too. Want to know how? Read on.

Target Words
These words will help you understand how science and sports are related.

- **energy:** the power to do work or cause a change

  Hitting a tennis ball in the center of your racket gives your return shot more energy.

- **momentum:** the energy of a moving body

  Running fast will give you the momemtum you need to tackle a bigger player.

- **physics:** the scientific study of matter and energy

  Physics can explain amazing skateboard tricks.

Reader Tips
Here's how to get the most out of this book.

- **Sidebars** Sidebars offer additional information about the topic covered in the book. The first sidebar is on page 21. It will tell you how your feet affect your ability to play different sports.

- **Reading for Detail** As you read, think about how the information answers the questions *who, what, where, when, why,* and *how.* These are the details. And they will help you to better understand what you read.

1

Football: Forces to Reckon With

What happens when two football players run into each other?

Crack! Bam! Ouch! There's a lot of power packed into a football tackle. It can bend arms and legs the wrong way and break bones if you're not careful. That's where a little science can be a big help—especially **physics.**

Physics is the scientific study of **matter** and **energy.** Matter is anything that has weight and takes up space—a chair, a desk, you. In this case, the matter that matters is a defensive back's shoulder and a fullback's body.

Energy is the ability of something to do work or to make things move. In this case, we're interested in the energy of the defensive back and the fullback who are headed for a collision.

In any collision, the player with the most energy has the edge. The energy of a moving body is called **momentum.** To figure out how much momentum something has, multiply its weight by its speed.

So, let's say you're a skinny defensive back trying to take out a bulked-up fullback. You can make up for the difference in weight by increasing your speed. Say you weigh 140 pounds and you're moving 10 miles an hour. The fullback weighs 200 pounds, but he's only moving 5 miles an hour. Who's got more momentum? You do! (Your momentum is 140 x 10 = 1,400; his momentum is 200 x 5 = 1,000.) By running faster, you create more energy than the fullback.

It may sound scary to speed up when you've got a huge fullback coming at you. But most players will tell you: The faster you move, the safer you are. "Whatever you do, don't slow down," says Jeremy Bernfeld, a high school lineman at Newton High North in Massachusetts. "When somebody runs at you, go full speed ahead. That's the best way to avoid injury." Jeremy's coach trains all his players in the science of sports.

Helmets reduce the risk of brain injury by 85 percent.

Use Your Head

Speed alone, however, will not keep you safe. In every collision, energy is transferred from one object to another. Players need to make sure that the energy transferred to them during a tackle doesn't injure their bodies.

The first line of defense is a helmet. Just ask David Halstead. He's a safety adviser for the National Football League. "During a football game, the players' heads get hit from all directions," Halstead explains. "The helmet's hard shell distributes energy from a hit to foam pads under the shell. If the pads can't absorb all the energy, the shell breaks apart. Breaking the shell uses up most of the energy from the hit. Very little energy is left over to damage the player's head."

"Helmets are the greatest buy on the market," adds Halstead. "They've been proven to reduce the risk of brain injury by 85 percent."

—Heads Up!—

What parts of a helmet help it absorb the energy of a collision?

Bull Your Neck

As good as helmets are, they can't absorb all the energy from a collision. So tacklers need to think about how their bodies will handle the rest of the impact.

"From day one, coaches tell you to 'bull your neck,'" high school lineman Jeremy explains. "Players pull up their shoulders and tip back their heads a little. It saves you from breaking your neck or getting a horrible spinal injury."

Jeremy is right. If you ram your opponent with your head down and your back straight, the impact will jam your spine. The spaces between your vertebrae (the bones that make up your spine) can absorb some of the impact. But a hard hit could break bones.

So remember, it's better to bend than to break. You have physics to thank for that.

Heads Up!

What can happen to the energy from a collision if a tackler leads with his head?

CHAPTER

Basketball: A Better Dribble

How do you make air bounce? Try pumping it into a basketball.

The ball goes into play with just six seconds left. The announcer calls the play-by-play. "Powell takes the inbound pass. She dribbles downcourt. She's in the lane. She lays it in!" BUZZZZZ. "The Shock team wins the game!"

Buzzer beaters like Elaine Powell know how to control a ball. She's the point guard for the Detroit Shock, one of the teams in the Women's National Basketball Association (WNBA).

As a point guard, Powell knows the importance of dribbling well. "Keep your head up and dribble low," she says. "If you don't, it's easy for another player to steal the ball."

11

Elaine Powell controls the ball by keeping her head up and dribbing low. Just try to steal it from her!

What are the forces at work when Powell puts the ball to the floor? And how can you use them to sharpen your game?

The Way the Ball Bounces

Drop a pillow or a book. What happens? Chances are it just hits the floor and stays there. That's **gravity** at work. Gravity pulls you toward the earth and keeps your feet on the ground. It also pulls pillows, books, and basketballs to the floor.

For an object to bounce, it needs a force, or energy, that can push against gravity. That energy comes from the speed and weight of the falling object. The question is: What happens to the energy when the object hits the ground?

A pillow is flexible and **porous.** When it lands, the energy that's created moves the foam or feathers around and pushes the air out of holes in the fabric. There's no energy left to push the pillow back up. When a book hits the floor, the energy is converted to vibrations. That's because the book is stiff and dense. You can see some of the vibration. You hear the rest as a loud thud!

A basketball, on the other hand, is filled with air, which is made up of gases. There's a lot of space between the tiny parts, or particles, that make up the gas. And there are no holes in the ball for the gas to escape through. Plus, the shell of the ball isn't stiff.

So when a basketball hits the floor, it changes shape. The gas particles are pushed closer together toward the bottom of the basketball. The gas that's pushed together, or compressed, works like a spring. It pushes away from the floor and up to the top of the basketball, pushing the basketball back into shape and into the air.

Pat, Don't Slap

How high a ball bounces depends on how it's made. And it depends on the force with which it is sent toward the ground. That's important for hard-charging dribblers like Powell and high school player Matt Westman.

Westman plays for the Newton North Tigers of Massachusetts. His coach, Paul Connolly, is the "Shot Doctor." He's taught professionals and college teams about the mechanics of basketball.

Westman's coach taught him to be gentle with the ball when dribbling. "Pat, don't slap," says Connolly. Slapping gives the ball more energy going down. That means it's got more energy coming up. The higher bounce gives opponents a better chance to steal the ball.

That's one reason why basketball players don't use volleyballs. A volleyball, which is meant to fly, is made of lighter material and has too much air inside it.

Westman, who also stars in volleyball, put both kinds of balls to the test. The volleyball, he decided, doesn't belong on the basketball court. "It bounces quicker, but way too high. This ball is an easy steal."

Then he picked up a basketball and tried to spike it. "Ouch," he laughed. "That really hurt my hand."

Heads Up!

Think of a baseball. Use the ideas in this chapter to predict whether it would bounce well or not. Then explain why.

Baseball: Watching for a Good Pitch

Now you see it. Now you don't.

Fastball pitchers pitch at speeds of over ninety miles per hour. They hurl heat. They throw smoke. They burn balls into home plate in less than four-tenths of a second. How does a batter's body and brain work together fast enough to handle all that speed?

That's where **biomechanics** comes to the rescue. It's the study of body movements.

In the Blink of an Eye

So how exactly do batters hit those fastballs? The first thing you'll hear from a batting coach is: "Keep your eye on the ball." That's good advice. But it's physically impossible. The eye can't follow a speeding ball all the way to the plate.

Batters can only watch the ball for two-tenths of a second after it leaves the pitcher's hand. After that, the ball is moving across their field of vision too quickly for their eyes to keep up.

So batters really have to pay attention during that brief split second when they can see the pitch. Most batters use about half that time to figure out the kind of pitch it is—fastball, curveball, slider, or knuckleball. That leaves one-tenth of second to decide whether it's in the strike zone.

In two-tenths of a second more, the pitch will reach home plate. The body has just one-tenth of a second to get ready, and a final tenth of a second to swing.

Here's the play-by-play of what happens inside a batter's body in that four-tenths of a second. First, a batter's eyes have to focus on the pitch, like a camera taking a close-up. Then the eyes send a series of snapshots to the brain.

Heads Up!

It takes a pitch four-tenths of a second to reach home plate. Why do batters only have half that time to decide to swing?

17

Alex Rodriguez looks for a good pitch. But his eye will have only about two tenths of a second to track it.

The brain thinks about these snapshots. It figures out what they mean and decides what to do with the pitch. Then it sends signals to the muscles. Swing. Don't swing. Or jump back so the ball doesn't hit you! That pitch is way inside!

Scientists call this process eye-brain-body **coordination.** The nerve cells in the eyes, brain, and body all work together. These cells, hundreds of thousands of them, send electronic messages to each other. The messages move at 250 miles per hour. A fast pitch might be 100 miles per hour.

So the nerve cells move quicker than the fastball. But they have a lot to do!

Beating the Ball

How do batters speed up the process? They save time by being **efficient.** Each batter finds the best way to use that short time.

---**Heads Up!**---
Think about what it takes for a batter to hit a ball. Has your opinion of baseball changed? Why or why not?

Some batters don't waste time guessing what kind of pitch is coming. "If I guessed, I might be too late," says Chicago Cubs slugger Sammy Sosa. "I look for strikes. I never look for pitches."

Batters also train their eyes to pick up the pitch from the moment it leaves the pitcher's hand. That leaves more time to get ready and to swing, if the pitch is a good one. To help batters focus, coaches tell them to "build a mental tunnel between you and the pitcher." Block out everything else. When the pitcher's free leg hits the ground, it's just you and the ball.

"You face hard throwers," says Cubs batting coach Gary Matthews, Sr., "and you have to look hard at what they throw."

Matthews knows another trick. It's called "practice, practice, and more practice." Batters swing at a lot of pitches. They watch pitchers throw at other batters. They train their brains to think faster.

And thinking fast can be the difference between a pop fly and a home run.

Athletes' Feet

It takes fast eyes and hands to hit a baseball. After that, you need fast feet to get around the bases. But not all feet are created equally. The way your feet are built—their **anatomy**—can make a big difference in the way you move.

Does your big toe stick out farther than your second one? If so, you can dig in and push off faster than other people. This gives you an edge in running bases or sprinting. But in distance running, a long big toe can cause pain that slows you down. It slaps the track over and over. This can cause the toe to break or bruise.

Flat feet help in sports with a lot of stops and turns, like tennis or basketball. When a greater area of your foot makes contact with the ground, you get more **traction.** You can plant your feet firmly and spin around fast.

Strong ankles make for strong skiing, boarding, or skating. But they don't help with swimming, where the ankle should be flexible.

Check out your feet. What kind of fancy footwork can they do?

Tennis:
What a Racket

One point is sweeter than the others.

Talk about double trouble. Venus and Serena Williams know how to raise a racket. Time and again, the swift-serving sisters have hammered at their opponents across the tennis court. They've got a "sweet spot" for success. It's found in the center of a tennis racket. When Venus and Serena hit this spot, they can bash balls at over 120 miles per hour.

What's the secret behind the sweet spot? Almost any physicist can tell you the answer.

All Strung Out

According to physicist and tennis expert Howard Brody, here's how it works. When Venus or Serena make contact with a ball, the energy

Serena hits the sweet spot of her racket. That gives her return shot more power.

from the collision gets transferred to the racket. That energy makes the strings stretch backward. As the strings stretch, they gain **potential energy,** or stored energy, just like a basketball when it hits the ground.

When the strings rebound, or bounce back, they release the energy and fire the ball back

23

through the air. "A racket's strings work like a little trampoline," explains Brody. Think about how a trampoline works. When you jump in the middle, you get a better bounce than near the sides. The same goes for the racket strings. "They're designed to give back 95 percent of the energy they store."

How much energy can a player make the strings store? That depends mainly on three things. First of all, speed creates energy. (Remember learning about momentum in Chapter 1?) So, the faster the racket and ball are moving, the more energy will be created when the ball hits the racket.

Second, stretchy strings create more energy. Some players loosen their strings to get more power. The loose strings stretch back farther and store more energy. But there are some trade-offs.

Heads Up!

Recall what happens when a basketball bounces. How does that compare to a ball bouncing off a tennis racket?

When loose strings stretch, they create a kind of pocket that the ball sinks into. The ball tends to rebound off the strings at a greater angle, making a player lose some control.

The third way to create more energy is to control the vibrations.

Good Vibrations

Some of the energy from a collision is expended in vibrations. If a racket vibrates a lot, it means the frame, and your arm, are absorbing energy. So players need to keep vibrations to a minimum. They want the maximum amount of energy to be transferred to the return shot.

That's where the sweet spot comes in. It's the place on a racket's strings that creates the fewest vibrations when the ball hits.

"Basically," says Brody, "it's where it feels good to hit the ball."

Most rackets have two sweet spots. One is right in the center. The other is about two inches away from the throat, where the handle begins. Hit a sweet spot, and you can feel the power. The ball seems to leap off your racket strings.

Miss the sweet spots, and the racket handle jumps or shakes. It's like trying to keep a jackhammer in place.

Venus and Serena are strong enough to handle that. But thanks to the sweet spot, they don't have to. Victory—how sweet it is.

—Heads Up!—

What are three things you can do to hit a tennis ball with more power?

Swimming:
No Resistance

Try putting a little science into your stroke.

Amy Van Dyken knows how to overcome **resistance.** That's any force that slows you down. She's overcome it in the swimming pool—and in life.

Van Dyken, an Olympic record holder, has asthma, a condition that can make breathing difficult. "To help me control it," says Van Dyken, "my doctor told me to take up swimming—a good exercise for the lungs."

At first, Van Dyken couldn't even swim the length of an Olympic-sized pool. She slowly improved with practice, but still, she didn't have much speed.

When she was in high school, she joined the swim team. "I was always the worst swimmer," laughs Van Dyken. "I kept swimming, losing, and trying again."

Some of her teammates felt she was hurting the team. They tried to discourage her. They told her to quit. "So I went out there and showed them," recalls Van Dyken.

But it wasn't just Van Dyken's attitude that won medals. It was her speed. She was getting stronger. And she had science on her side.

Don't Be a Drag

Water is 733 times denser, or thicker, than air. That means it's 733 times harder to move through. So swimmers like Van Dyken find ways to reduce the **drag.** Drag is the slowing down of an object as it moves through a substance. Think of dropping a spoon into a jar of honey. That's drag.

"An important way to reduce drag on a swimmer is to focus on body position," says swim scientist Scott Riewald.

Van Dyken tries to keep her body horizontal, or flat. That way there is less body surface

**Olympic champion Amy Van Dyken knows how to
overcome resistance.**

© Tony Duffy/Getty Images

meeting the water as she moves through the pool.
She also tries to keep herself close to the surface
so less of her body has to cope with the heavy
drag of the water.

Slick Tricks

The human body has a lot of bumps and hairs that increase **friction** with the water. Friction is the main cause of drag. Hair also adds weight. It absorbs up to 15 times its weight in water. While that may not amount to much, every ounce increases the load a swimmer has to carry through the water. So, many swimmers shave off their body hair. It's been proven to take about a second off a swimmer's time over a hundred meters.

Swimmers also cover their heads with tight caps and wear full-length, high-tech bathing suits. These suits, known as fast-suits, let water flow more smoothly over their bodies.

Swimmers are always looking for ways to reduce drag. They often train in a tow. This machine pulls them 5 percent faster than they swim. It gives swimmers a chance to discover techniques that reduce drag at faster speeds.

Heads Up!

Look up friction *in the glossary. List three kinds of friction you come across every day.*

Swimming Against the Tide

But reducing friction is only half the story. Swimming strongly is the other half. To make swimmers stronger, Olympic trainers put them in flumes, machines that create strong currents. Swimmers swim against the currents until their lungs and muscles ache. They want to get strong. But they don't want bulky muscles.

Muscle is denser than water, which means it tends to sink. Fat, on the other hand, is less dense than water. So it tends to float. To keep themselves high in the water, where there's less drag, swimmers want to keep some fat on their bodies.

For Van Dyken, the attention to scientific detail paid off. She's won five Olympic gold medals—four of them at age twenty-three, just ten years after she first dove for her dream. That's definitely not a drag.

Marathon Running: Going the Distance

On your mark! Get set! Go!

Imagine running 105 laps around a track without stopping. Now imagine doing it at 72 seconds per lap. Keep going at that pace for 2 hours, 5 minutes, and 38 seconds. If you can do this, you will match the world record for running a marathon.

So do you think you have what it takes? You might. Not everyone is built for speed. Some bodies are built for distance. Which type are you? Your muscle fibers help determine that.

Muscles are made up of two types of fibers. They can be either fast-twitch or slow-twitch.

Fast-twitch fibers contract (tighten) and relax quickly. But they tire easily. So they're not good for endurance sports like running a marathon. However, they're great for explosive sports, like sprinting or lifting weights.

Slow-twitch fibers take up to ten times longer to contract and relax. They're slow, but steady. They give you the energy for sports, like long-distance running or climbing a mountain.

"A great marathoner has a very large percentage of slow-twitch fibers," says Dr. Greg Diamond, a member of the American College of Sports Medicine.

Does that mean only "slow-twitchers" should run marathons? "No," says Diamond. "Marathons are for everyone. But nature gives people with a lot of slow-twitch muscles an edge."

Fuel to Burn

How do those slow-twitch muscles get the energy they need to last through a marathon? They get it from a **chemical reaction** known as aerobic respiration.

In aerobic respiration, your muscles use oxygen to turn nutrients from food into a chemical called ATP (adenosine triphosphate). ATP provides the energy to power muscle cells.

During this marathon race, Khalid Khannouchi burned about 100 calories per mile.

Distance runners need to make sure they have enough fuel to make this reaction happen. They get it from **calories,** the energy stored in food.

"A typical runner burns about 100 calories per mile," explains Diamond. "Do the math for a marathon. We're talking about more than 2,600 calories. Compare that with the 1,200 to 2,000 calories most people need a day."

Eat for the Long Haul

Protein, fat, and carbohydrates are all sources of calories. But protein and fat are harder to digest than carbohydrates. So they don't supply fuel quickly enough.

The best way to store up fuel for a race, Diamond says, is to "carbo-load."

Runners carbo-load by eating a lot of carbohydrates. Fruit is a good source of carbohydrates. So are starchy foods like pasta, grains, and potatoes.

The body turns carbohydrates to glycogen, a kind of sugar. With the help of oxygen, the glycogen is turned into ATP and stored in muscle cells for energy during a race.

Most top distance runners are also champion eaters. They usually start carbo-loading about four days before a race. Most trainers suggest eating about 65 percent carbohydrates. The idea is to store enough glycogen so it doesn't run out during a race. When that happens, muscles start burning fat, which takes more energy. That's when marathoners "hit the wall." Their muscles run low on fuel, and they slow down to a crawl.

"I don't hit the wall today," says Diamond. "But I did in early marathons. Suddenly, you feel like you're moving through molasses."

So next time you want to push yourself, make sure to put enough fuel in the tank. Otherwise, you could hit the wall, too. Ouch!

Heads Up!

Why do runners "hit the wall"? What happens in their body to cause it?

Fight or Flight?
Your Body Doesn't Care

Your body doesn't recognize the cause of stress. It doesn't know if you're running from a lion or running toward a finish line. But either way, when your body knows you're under stress, it tries to help out.

Here's what happens. The brain tells your adrenal glands to produce a chemical called epinephrine. It's also known as adrenaline.

Adrenaline is a powerful **stimulant.** It gives your body what it needs to help you fight or run. It speeds your breathing. Your heart pounds, forcing blood carrying oxygen and sugar to your muscles, and your brain.

Adrenaline is no substitute for training. But it can help in a pinch.

Climbing: Reaching New Heights

Could you make it to the top of the world?

Climbers call Everest "Big E." At 29,035 feet, it's the world's tallest mountain. What does it take to stand on the top of the world? It takes clear lungs, a strong heart, lots of guts, and most of all, experience.

Does that mean you'll never reach a peak like Everest? No. But you need to know what you're getting into and train for it. Climbers push their bodies to the limit.

Thin Air

The biggest problem climbers face can be summed up in two words: oxygen **deprivation.** Every step up Everest takes climbers to a higher altitude, or height above sea level. The higher they go, the less gravity there is to hold the **atmosphere** down. So the atmosphere, which is made up of gases, thins out. One of those gasses is oxygen, the stuff we breathe.

The air at the top of Everest has about one-third the oxygen content as the air at sea level. Many climbers say that getting near the top feels like having one of their lungs ripped out.

What happens when oxygen supplies get low? The body goes into emergency mode. Breathing rates go up to get more oxygen into the lungs. Heart rates also soar. The heart pumps more blood, which picks up oxygen from the lungs and carries it to the muscles and the brain.

All this added activity means the body has to work a lot harder than it normally does. "It feels like you're running around a football field," says Stacy Allison, the first U.S. woman to climb Everest. "And that's when you're resting."

As a result, you must consume more fuel in the form of food. At sea level, most people need less than two thousand calories a day. Climbers need to put away between seven thousand and nine thousand during the same 24 hours.

"We lick cubes of butter like lollipops," says Allison. "Yet, as much as we try to eat, many climbers still lose fifteen to twenty percent of their body weight."

A Gift for Altitude

Some climbers are better suited for altitude than others. Stacy Allison and Ed Viesturs, who's climbed Everest five times, are what one scientist calls "aerobic marvels." Their muscles use oxygen very efficiently.

Viesturs also has a big lung capacity. That means his lungs can hold more air than the average person's.

Viesturs and Allison were born with certain advantages. But training can have a huge effect on aerobic capacity.

Most climbers run or bike regularly. This kind of training causes two important things to happen. First, the heart gets stronger and pumps more blood with each beat. That means it doesn't have to pump as many times. Second, the muscles learn to use less oxygen to produce the same amount of ATP.

©Zefa Visual Media/Index Stock Imagery

Climbers can lose fifteen to twenty percent of their body weight.

Training helps climbers get ready for Everest. But nothing is more important than experience. Climbers get to know their bodies and help each other listen for signs of distress. "We're constantly asking, 'How are you feeling?'" Allison says. "If the answer isn't right or if a person acts strangely, we come down. No summit is worth a life."

Heads Up!

Climbers and distance runners train in similar ways. Why?

Feeling the Pressure

If pressure lightens up when you climb, what do you suppose happens when you dive deep into the ocean?

Sylvia Earle knows. A deep-sea diver, Earle once strapped herself to the nose of a special submarine and dove 1,250 feet under the ocean's surface. Then Earle unstrapped herself and walked around the ocean floor. The weight of the ocean put six hundred pounds of pressure on every square inch of her body. That's about forty times the pressure you feel walking around on land.

Earle wore a special suit to protect herself from the body-crushing pressure. The suit also prevented oxygen from being squeezed out of her lungs and muscles.

Next, Earle wants to be dropped into the Marianas Trench. At 35,800 feet, it's the deepest spot in the ocean. In 2003, submersibles, or deep-water submarines, could only go down 20,000 feet. But Earle is helping to develop a machine that will one day make the dive.

Skateboarding: Going Airborne

Ride a concrete wave. Catch big air. But remember—what goes up must come down.

Tony Hawk, one of the skateboarding greats, knows how to fly. He's the master of "sick tricks," skateboard talk for gravity-defying moves. He invented the 900—a move that involves two and a half flips.

Hawk says, "People always ask, 'How does the board stick to your feet?'" He's got a quick answer for them. "It's just the ollie," Hawk explains.

Oh, is that all? Hawk might as well have said it's just magic.

The ollie is the basic move that allows skaters to get airborne. Watching one leaves most people scratching their heads. Skaters jump into the air from flat ground without grabbing the board.

There's nothing tying their feet to the board, yet it stays glued to their sneakers.

How do they do it? It's no mystery to physicists.

Ollie Physics

The ollie is all about force and friction. Force is anything that tends to push an object, either setting it in motion or changing its direction. Friction, as you know, is the resistance created when one object rubs against another.

When skaters start an ollie, there are three forces at work on the board. Gravity is pushing down. So is the weight of a skater, on both the front and back of the board. The ground, on the other hand, is pushing up. All these forces cancel each other out, and the skateboard just rolls along.

Then the fun begins. Use the pictures on page 46 to help you figure out how Hawk does it.

1. Go Low. First, Hawk bends his knees and crouches low. He gets more force with bent, rather than straight, knees. (Try jumping with straight legs.) Crouching also lowers his **center of gravity**, or balancing point, so he doesn't fall off the board.

1 Go Low.

2 Go High.

3 Slam It.

4 Time It.

5 Stick It.

These pictures can help you understand the process.

© Tony Donaldson/Icon Sports Media

"The center of gravity is located about two inches below your belly button," says Dr. Bill Robertson, a skater and physicist whose nickname is Dr. Skateboard. "Skaters try to keep it over the middle of the board and as close to the board as possible."

2. Go High. Now Hawk is ready to jump. He straightens his back leg and exerts a force on the tail of the board. The front leg stays bent, taking force off the front of the board. That causes the board to pivot, or tip, lifting the front wheels off the ground.

3. Slam It. The force of Hawk's back leg slams the tail of the board into the ground. The energy from the collision forces the tail back up. Once airborne, Hawk applies a little friction. With the nose pointed up, he slides his front foot up the scratchy grip tape on the nose. This helps to raise the board further.

—Heads Up!—
What finally makes a skateboard leave the ground during an ollie?

4. Time It. Hawk pulls his knees to his chest. He also pushes down on his front foot to level out the board. That brings the rear of the board up even further. If Hawk times this right, his back foot rises at the same rate as the tail of the board. That's what makes it look like the board is stuck to his feet.

5. Stick It. Gravity always wins in the end. The upward forces from the jump are only strong enough to keep Hawk airborne for a couple of seconds. Then gravity pulls Hawk and the board down at the same rate. Then Hawk bends his knees to absorb the impact of the landing.

Hawk's moves may look like magic. But even he can't defy gravity. After all, it's just an ollie. And what makes it work is physics.

Speed Skating:
Getting an Edge

**_They move at speeds over thirty miles
per hour. How do they do it?_**

Imagine gliding swiftly across a smooth sheet of ice. The cold air rushes past you. The noises around you blend into one big "whoosh." You have become one with nature. You've also become something else.

There's a saying in the sport of speed skating. "When you speed skate, you become something you study in physics class."

Speed skaters live by the laws of physics. One of the most important laws goes like this. Objects in motion stay in motion unless acted on by an outside force. In other words, if nothing gets in the way of a moving object, it will keep moving at a constant speed.

That might sound like good news for a speed skater. There's just one problem. There's no place on earth where an object can move without something getting in the way.

Every moving thing runs into resistance, even when you can't see the cause. Like swimmers in the water, skaters face drag. It comes from wind resistance. The tiniest particles in the air push against their bodies as they try to whip around the track.

Speed skaters try to limit wind drag by crouching down, with their arms tucked behind their backs. They wear special suits so the air flows over their bodies. "They try to punch as small a hole as possible into the air in front of them," says Paul Marchese, an adviser to the U.S. Olympic speed skating team.

Friction, or rubbing movement, between the ice and their skate blades is another cause of drag. That's why speed skaters and hockey players like what is known as fast ice. It's hard, cold, smooth, and easy to glide across. Figure skaters like slow ice. It's soft, warm, snowy, and easy to grip for difficult jumps and spins.

"Making ice for each sport is a science," says Marchese. "The ice makers control the thickness. They also control the temperature of the concrete floor below the ice. Speed skaters look for thin ice kept as cold and as hard as possible. We don't want our blades to sink into the ice."

Staying on Track

Skaters do what they can to increase their speed. But they need control as well. They move at speeds of more than 30 miles an hour.

"The sensation of speed is almost like no other sport," explains Marchese. "You hit a curve and think, 'There's no way I can come out of this.' But you do."

The skaters' momentum tends to carry them straight forward, even when they hit a curve. But skaters have a few tricks for staying on the track. They keep a low center of gravity, or balance point. They also lean severely into the turn. That way the force of their body weight pushes in against the force of their forward momentum.

Finally, skaters use special equipment. Their skate blades are longer and thinner than the

**Apolo Anton Ohno had to lean into this turn. His weight counters
the momentum that would carry him straight ahead.**

blades on hockey skates or figure skates. The length gives skaters more contact with the ice. The thin blade helps cut a tiny groove in the ice that holds speed skaters in place on the turns. It gives them traction.

All this science helps top skaters get a feel for the ice that can't be described in scientific terms.

"I can feel it under my feet. I can feel it under my toes," says Apolo Anton Ohno, the Olympic short-track champion. "I feel every ripple in the ice. And I feel that's something that contributes to my success."

Heads Up!

List three things that help speed skaters stay on the track.

Glossary

anatomy *(noun)* the structure of a living organism or part of an organism (p. 21)

atmosphere *(noun)* the mixture of gasses that surround a planet (p. 39)

biomechanics *(noun)* the study of how the body moves (p. 16)

calorie *(noun)* the amount of heat energy food can produce as it passes through the body (p. 35)

center of gravity *(noun)* balancing point (p. 45)

chemical reaction *(noun)* what happens when two or more chemicals mix (p. 33)

coordination *(noun)* the ability of parts to work together (p. 19)

deprivation *(noun)* the lack of something (p. 38)

drag *(noun)* the slowing down of an object as it moves through a substance such as water or air (p. 28)

efficient *(adjective)* performing or functioning without wasting time or effort (p. 19)

energy *(noun)* the power to do work or cause a change (p. 6)

friction *(noun)* the rubbing of the surface of one object against another (p. 30)

gravity *(noun)* the force that attracts small objects to extremely large, dense objects, like planets or stars (p. 13)

matter *(noun)* the material or materials that makes up everything in the physical world (p. 6)

momentum *(noun)* the energy of a moving body (p. 7)

physics *(noun)* the scientific study of matter and energy (p. 6)

porous *(adjective)* full of holes (p. 13)

potential energy *(noun)* stored energy or energy that has not yet been released (p. 23)

resistance *(noun)* any force that slows motion or makes it harder to move (p. 27)

stimulant (noun) a substance that makes you move faster (p. 37)

traction *(noun)* the friction that keeps a moving body from slipping (p. 21)

Index

A

adrenaline 37

aerobic respiration 33

B

baseball 16–20

basketball 11–15

E

eye-brain-body
coordination 19

F

fast-twitch muscles
32–33

feet, anatomy of 21

football 6–10

friction 30–31, 45, 47, 50

G

glycogen 35–36

gravity 12–14, 39, 44–48,
51

M

marathons 32–36

momentum 7, 24–25, 51

mountain climbing
38–42

P

potential energy 24–25

R

resistance 27–31

S

skateboarding 44–48

slow-twitch muscles
32–33

speed skating 49–53

sweet spot 22–26

swimming 27–31

T

tennis 22–26